Animal

by Leonie Bennett

Editorial consultant: Mitch Cronick

Copyright © **ticktock Entertainment Ltd 2006**
First published in Great Britain in 2006 by **ticktock Media Ltd.,**
Unit 2, Orchard Business Centre, North Farm Road, Tunbridge Wells, Kent TN2 3XF

We would like to thank: Shirley Bickler and Suzanne Baker

ISBN 1 86007 976 8 pbk
Printed in China

Picture credits
t=top, b=bottom, c=centre, l-left, r=right, OFC= outside front cover
Corbis: 11, 12-13. Superstock: 4, 5, 6, 15, 16, 17, 19, 20, 21.

Every effort has been made to trace the copyright holders, and we apologise in advance for any
unintentional omissions. We would be pleased to insert the appropriate acknowledgements in any
subsequent edition of this publication.

A CIP catalogue record for this book is available from the British Library. All rights reserved. No part
of this publication may be reproduced, copied, stored in a retrieval system or transmitted in any form
or by any means electronic, mechanical, photocopying, recording or otherwise without prior
written permission of the copyright owner.

CONTENTS

I'm a vet

My name's Sam

I'm a vet.

4

Julia is a vet too.

Julia and I look after sick animals at an animal hospital.

The animals we see

Here are some of the animals we look after.

Small dogs

Big dogs

Guinea pigs

Rabbits

Parrots

Sometimes people bring lost animals to the hospital.

This cat is lost.

Cat

He is very hungry.

We give him food.

We will try to find his owners.

The things we use

We use all these things in our work.

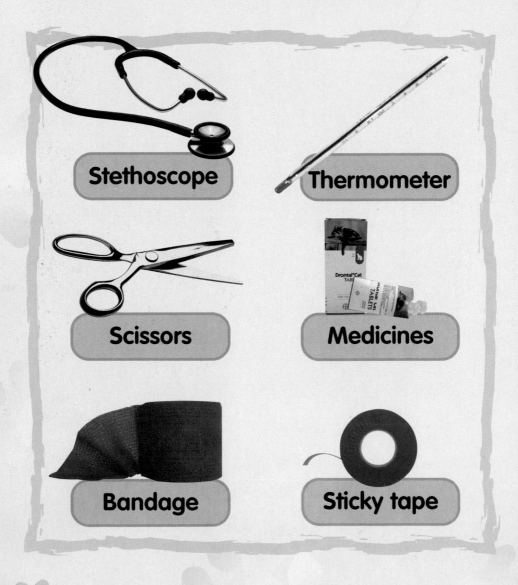

Stethoscope

Thermometer

Scissors

Medicines

Bandage

Sticky tape

This x-ray shows the bones in a cat's tail and legs.

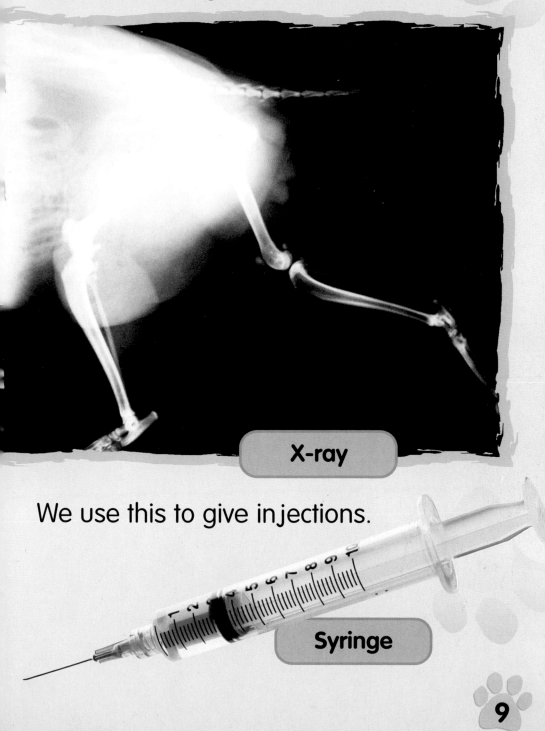

X-ray

We use this to give injections.

Syringe

Helping animals

This dog has
a bad paw.

We will do an
x-ray to check
her paw.

This dog has
a cut on his leg.

We will check to see
if it is OK.

Flea powder

This cat has fleas in her fur.

We will put powder on the cat's fur.

The powder will kill the fleas.

Injections

Many pets come to have injections.

The injections stop them getting ill.

Syringe

This kitten is seven weeks old.
She is having her first injection.

It does not hurt!

13

Alfie's story

This dog's name is Alfie.

Alfie is not well.

I feel his tummy.

I listen to his heart with a stethoscope.

The nurse helps.

Nurse

Stethoscope

15

Alfie's bad ear

I look in Alfie's eyes.

I look in his ears.

Ear drops

Alfie has a bad ear.

I put some drops in his ear to make it better.

I give Alfie a big collar.

Now Alfie can't scratch his ear.

Good boy, Alfie!

Suzie's check-up

Suzie is an old dog.

She has come for a check-up.

Julia checks how hot or cold Suzie is. She uses a thermometer.

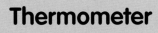

Thermometer

Stethoscope

Julia listens to Suzie's heart
with a stethoscope.

Good girl, Suzie!

Julia looks at Suzie's teeth.

She puts Suzie on the scales.

Suzie is not ill but she is too fat.

Scales

She must not eat so many
dog sweets.

Good girl, Suzie!

Yes or no?
At the animal hospital

This cat was lost.

Yes or no?

This dog had a bad ear.

Yes or no?

Suzie is an old dog.

Yes or no?

Alfie had a bad eye.

Yes or no?

Would you like to be a vet?

Why?

Activities

What did you think of this book?

 Brilliant    Good    OK

Which page did you like best? Why?

• • • • • • • • • • • • •

Which is the odd one out? Why?

stethoscope • cat • bandage

• • • • • • • • • • • • •

Make a 'Thank you' card to send to a vet who helped your pet.

• • • • • • • • • • • • •

Who is the author of this book? Have you read *Airline Pilot* by the same author?

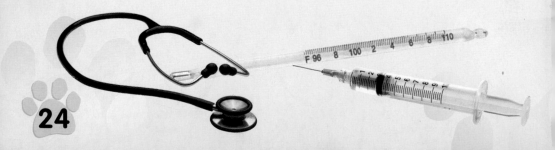